HOW TO IDENTIFY GREAT BUSINESS OPPORTUNITIES

➜A perfect guide to choosing the right and profitable business that is best for you

DAVID ALFORD

TABLE OF CONTENT

Dedication

Dedicated to my doggie….a fun loving puppy

CHAPTER ONE

Introduction

Anyone who is able to comprehend and act upon opportunities is one who succeeds in life. We discuss too much about being there at the right time, but what exactly does this actually mean? What happens to those that aren't there at the right time and at the appropriate place? Don't they get their opportunities?

So you are welcome to know how to understand business opportunities and make the most of them in your life.

You are welcome to figure out the best way to find and know the right business opportunities and take advantage of them in your life.

CHAPTER TWO

Business Opportunities – Do you know the Qualities of an Excellent Business Opportunity?

The first step of any successful business is to check out the quality of the business opportunity you want to begin. You should know what you must look for.

Listed below are several qualities that before you star any business you should assess. There are more, needless to say, but these will be the ones which you ought to definitely not miss out on:

1. The business should have targeted customer base.

What do we mean by that? Let's say you happen to be about to begin a home based business. Let's assume you are required to choose a business that is more in demand. Where demand is high and supply is less, you might have a much better range of succeeding. Consider the case of Search Engine Optimization opportunities for freelancers. It is possible to do this from home with no high investment. In this opportunity, the requirement on your own part is high and you are bound to do well if you put in the right effort, because the professionals here are fewer. You need such an opportunity.

2. The business ought to possess a breakeven point that is good. In case your business doesn't have that, you then should get substantial quantity of working capital. Building a project report that tells when and just how much you'll get in the business, and how much you'll need to put in, is an excellent idea.

3. Your interest with the business you have started is tremendously significant.

You can find a lot of people who started a business looking at its possibility, but don't reach the level they want, mainly because they don't have a lot of interest in the business.

4. Have the right resources on ground

Before starting with your intending business opportunity, see to it that you have the right resources on ground such as man power, guidance, consulting, monetary credit if necessary, infrastructure, etc. before you start out.

5. Check the competitiveness

Check to know if the business opportunity is extremely competitive or over in demand, if competition is very high, it will be difficult for you to get established in the business soon.

So, in summary, before you begin any business, you should test out all of the pluses and minuses of the business opportunity. It could possibly get very hard to quit after you've begin. Being forewarned is being better-equipped.

CHAPTER THREE

Where to Search for Business Opportunities?

Now that you know what to look out for in a business opportunity, it's also advisable to understand where to discover them, get more and new ideas. So just keep on reading, I will tell you the exact strategies on the best way to find business opportunities that are the best.

Strategy 1 - Search Engines: Your Gold Mine of Information

Search engines like Google are the most effective way to get information for just about any business. It is possible for you to say search engines are gold mines of information. You can do a common search and learn about a large number of business opportunities. But, needless to say, you wouldn't understand which of all these are great to embark on and which aren't, in which case, you might need to certainly read their reviews too, which again you will find through search engines. Look for specific forums on business opportunities where you will find people talking about them and giving their opinions.

Strategy 2 – Join Business Newsgroups or Forums (Online and Offline)

Newsgroups are now a day's quite in demand particularly online. There are lots of business forums having around 2 to 3 million users. Using forums, you will be able to discuss and get guidance from experts and from people who are seeking business opportunities as well. Just Google they keyword of your business with the word "forums" (e.g. baking "forums") and you will get list of top forums in that niche.

Strategy 3 - Classified Ads (Don't Overlook This)

Regularly check newspapers, TV news, online news, online press release where daily bases thousands of business opportunities are posted. Just take the advantage of this revolution and get great ideas for best business opportunities.

Strategy 4 – Get Memberships into Top Clubs

Clubs are one among the greatest places where people go for entertainment and as well share their business experiences and resources. Go for get-togethers so you could get lots of business ideas and great opportunities. Be into a social life and see how you can grow your business with new business opportunities.

Strategy 5 – Get Info from Government Bodies

Many great business opportunities are provided by authorities when it comes to leads, advice, help, grants and a number of other resources. This source is just one of the very trustworthy source than others. Simply get in touch with your local business management bodies to get an extended set of concepts and business information.

CHAPTER FOUR

Successful Persons Aren't Created Successful; They Understand and Accept New Opportunities

No one is born successful. When we were born we even don't understand the way to spell successful, understanding its significance is something rather far off. As and when we grow up, we start chipping in attempts to turn our lives into successful people. A number of us do achieve the success that we have thought about, but that doesn't come without a great deal of effort.

One of the most important ingredients in becoming successful is to have a vision, a dream. In case you don't understand the best way to dream, you'll most likely not attain anything in life. Many people are scared to dream, believing they'd be very frustrated should they not reach their aims. However, the truth is the fact that if you don't dream, you won't likely get it. Great people dreamt of going to the moon, flying and so on... you see now that we can fly and can equally can to the moon.

In this age when people are thinking the best way to construct gadgets that could turn object and even people invisible, it is very unwise to limit one's ideas. What do you really dream about? Likely you dream about purchasing a house or a car of your own or having an excellent business. In the light of all the achievements that people have made, do you still believe that it is as tough as you think? This demonstrates there isn't anything impossible in this world if you do it the right way, take initiatives and plan it properly.

Simply take the example of Bill Gates, our favorite example actually. Almost the entire world now uses his Microsoft products, not understanding that the products belong to an person who is a computer dropout. Also take a look at Facebook. It started as a college project and has today made a revolution in the field of social networking. Can we not talk about Google, which began in a dingy office and now it controls our online world. All these successes were achieved in just a few years!

So, don't lose hope, hold on to your big dreams and attempt to reach them. The simple measures which you must take are hard work, and to be there at the right time along with the perfect time. Follow this and no one can stop you from reaching your targets. Before performing them, plan things correctly on paper. Make milestones for yourself and give yourself rewards once reach there.

CHAPTER FIVE

Why We Should Forever Be On The Move!

I have observed a huge number of people failing in lives as a result of just one motive, i.e. they don't take actions. Let's say you have $10 million but you don't know how and where to use them. The money will become useless to you then. So, in case you have advice, resources and business plan, make it a point to execute them then. Don't just keep them on paper.

A lot of people work really hard during the first phases of their business, but when they don't succeed early on, they quit. You need to understand that success most likely won't come immediately. You occasionally work for a long time to get actual success and need to be dedicated and sometimes work for years to get real success. However, many people get tired very quickly. Most of these people never planned for the worst and they don't have back up plans. Keep all these things ready and keep working in your strategies and you will see that you've moved closer to success.

Failure isn't the only reason people quit working. In some people, overconfidence becomes the primary cause. All these are the people succeeded earlier on, but they become overconfident about their accomplishments, which makes them contented. They start thinking they have achieved everything and now they don't need to do much, but the fact is we should never stop and should always be on the move to achieve more and more success.

Then, there are several types of people who just keep dreaming, keep thinking they will do one thing or the other, but the truth is that we simply need to carry out those plans and not just to keep thinking. Everyone can dream but only those who work hard can achieve those dreams.

CHAPTER SIX

The Best Way To Identify Business Opportunities And Make Use Of Them Properly

There ought to be a formula to make a great successful business and plan to take actions on that formula which should carried out properly by acting upon them.

There are a couple of things that you should take care of which will help you to take action on your plan.

- Always anticipate for the best
- Make your work strategy on paper
- Dedicate yourself to work and finish the job on time
- Make milestone for your strategy
- Create schedules for daily, weekly and monthly task and don't overlook them
- Always keep a backup plan which will keep you in the business

Sometimes we work really hard but at the end of the day we are not satisfied with our work and if we observe properly, we will realize we have achieved nothing. In the event you work with no strategies. This happens if you work without a plan. So always make a complete plan on paper.

Give yourself gifts and goals too. We always need some sort of motivation to maintain our self with great standing in business. Let's say you needed to finish a job by tomorrow evening but you finished it in the morning, then you have to reward yourself.   give yourself some benefit. This increases your self esteem, which is very important.

Organize your job with backup plans, say you're unable to complete the job on time for virtually any reason then you should have plan what to do to cover the time. Always prioritize your tasks. Sequence them in the order of their significance. There should to be a "must-do job" for weekly or daily basis. This gives you the opportunity to complete your important work at least in a week if you don't skip any schedule.

If you don't understand the way to create a plan, get assistance from professionals including accountants and other financial experts, but don't start with no strategies. 90% of businesses fail because they don't have any plan on paper. At the same time, executing the plan is of ultimate value too.

CHAPTER SEVEN

Does Opportunities Hit Twice?

There is a saying that failure is a step toward success. Many people quit when they've failed once. They fall victims of failure thinking that if they've failed once, they won't have the ability to do well again. However, opportunity do recur in life; you just have to be ready and grab them when they come again. You should not opt out of accepting these opportunities when they come by you again.

Nine in ten of the people who are successful now were once confronted by failure sometime in their lives. Francis Ford Coppola was a washout when his important directorial business was said to be insignificant when it was launched. But he continued his attempts unrelenting, and that "insignificant is known today as the classic Godfather. A person of average mindset would have given up when people become cynical, but he didn't and he gave us one of our greatest cinematic masterpieces. This is only a learning process.

When we began schooling in childhood, we didn't know a lot of things. We learned everything by making mistakes and fixing them. That is part of our success. If you've failed before, you will be more successful as you will know what to do if you are faced with that kind of challenge in the future.

So it matters not if we've lost the opportunity twice or more, it keeps coming. I'd like to give a practical example. Let's say you were waiting for a bus to go somewhere and for some reasons, you missed one bus, what will you really do? Just give up? Won't you strive for another bus to reach your destination or will you return to where you were coming from? Just as you wait for the bus and catch up the next time it arrives, same way you should wait for opportunities as well. And, just like buses do, opportunities come by you again as well.

If your time and efforts are well-meaning and right, there's absolutely no reason you must not succeed in life, but you need to be prepared to accept these in the right way, and certainly you'll have the ability to handle them nicely as you've learned a lot of things from your previous failures.

So never get overly depressed, keep trying your best and you'll be scaling new heights of success some day.

CHAPTER EIGHT

Utilizing the World Wide Web to "Find" Your Business Opportunities

The internet is among the most effective places to find business opportunities; there are lots of choices available there where you can collect data, research, research papers and so forth. We're going to discuss about some of the top techniques to discover what is more in demand and what people are searching for.

1. You can do research on almost any product or service using search engines.

It's possible for you to find how many competitors there, what they are promoting, how long they have into business, what their USP is, at what cost they sell and so forth. You can quickly get all the info that is needed from search engine. Just enter your keyword and you get the advice and information that you need.

2. You Can Try Google Trends.

This tool helps you to see the demand and how the graph is going on. For instance, you can know regarding iPhone, what was the trend in 2006, 2007 or now, in this way you can easily know how the product or service is in demand in last the few years which will help you decide.

3. You can try eBay, Amazon and other listing sites.

These sites give details of which product or business is more in demand, the products that users are searching for, what people are buying and so forth. If you go to all these websites you'll be able to know which products are highlighted as these sites will only show products or service that is in present demand, so their so we can use their ideas.

4. You can use Google External Keyword tool.

This tool will give you overall search volume of a any keyword of your choice which people are searching for. For instance, the keyword "weight loss" was searched for 30,400,000 times in just one month by only American users.

So, you see there are many ways to get information on different business opportunities. Just search it.

CHAPTER NINE

Listening to an opportunity Isn't Just Enough; You Must Get It into Actions

When you work for someone it makes it really simple for you, usually they take all the risk, guide you, advise you things to do and how to do them but when you opt to begin your personal business it's entirely a new game. The main part to start any business, either entrepreneurship or online business you are required to take actions, yes actions and actions. You should not only need to plan on what to do, when to do it and how to do it but also implement the plan you have made. As it is your business, you only have to take action, no one else will do that for you.

Some of the very important reasons why most people are not making it in life is lack commitment to their business, zero hard work. You need to execute your plan immediately. Mere thinking of an opportunity with no plans and actions to implement it is not going to take you anywhere. If you work hard and execute your plans as per planned, you will definitely be rewarded as expected and many times much more than expected.

There is a saying that actions speaks louder than words. So put your actions into plan and see how it gives you return. You don't get anything simply by thinking about it or speaking it out; you really need to take actions. It's not all that difficult to be a go getter or put your plans into action, just be confident, committed to yourself and you will see the results in no time.

There's endless potential for hardworking people and for those who put their plans in action and not just listening to an opportunity.

CHAPTER TEN

Inspiring People That Will Help You Achieve Your Targets

Attaining your target just isn't as tough as many matters. In the event you follow a few of the most popular techniques from actual life, it's possible for you to achieve your target. I want to show you one very simple example of "word of mouth" advertising technique. Let's say you must obtain a T.V that which you are doing? Request your friends what TV is the most effective? Get reviews online? Get expert guidance? Right? We do all this before purchasing or taking actions. This can be actually quite straightforward advertising technique of involving more and more visitors to assist you boost your organization. When they enjoy the item or service they'll surly encourage it to others with no cost as they would like to provide their family and friends the top.

Reaching your goal is not as difficult as many thinks. You can reach your goal if you follow some of the common techniques from real life. Let me show you one very simple example of "word of mouth" marketing technique. Let's say you want to buy a television set.

What you do?

Ask your friends the best television out there?

Get reviews online?

Get expert advice right?

Yes we do all these before buying or taking action and it is really very simple marketing technique of involving more and more people to help you promote your business. If they liked the product or service you provided, they will surely recommend it to others with no cost as they would like to provide their family and friends the best quality product out there.

Take for instance MLM. It is totally based on "word of mouth" marketing. One person joins the network and invites others to join and then others invite more people and the chain continues. Through this way, the company reaches its target easily without much marketing and only concentrate on the quality of their product.

You too can follow this same method, join more and more hubs and events and spread your network. The more networks of people you have, the more easily you can reach your goals. You indirectly help them and they also do the same. It is a kind of a win win situation. Can anything be better than this?

So start joining different hubs, clubs, groups, events, parties, tours and make friends and reach your goals easily with no stress.

CHAPTER ELEVEN

CONCLUSION: Don't Quit with Just a Single Opportunity

I can claim and maintain that 99% of people don't get satisfied with what they have. For instance, a person who has a bicycle will want a motorcycle, those who already have a car will want a luxury car, those who have luxury car will wants to have a private jet and so on. This is the nature of humans and that's why we are so much successful as we always have dreams that keep us going on.

So when you have so many dreams, do you think it can be completed with just one successful opportunity or business? When we want everything, why don't we try to grab more and more opportunities which will give us everything we need in life? The truth is most worlds' richest people have multiple streams of income from several businesses. Most of them started with one business and now have multiple businesses to their names. We think that by investing some amount and getting good returns that everything is fine; but the fact still remains that we always need more and so that we can have more and more business opportunities and more income too.

The Burger King started with only a single restaurant but now it has franchisees all around the globe. This is the power of perseverance, looking for opportunities and acting on them. If you stop at any point you are not going to fulfill the dreams of becoming rich and famous. Diversification is a very important aspect of getting to your destination.

Lastly, Opportunities come everyone's way but not many people understand what they should do with them. And most people don't even know where to look for the right opportunities.

But now you have a start and the right motivation. So now go forth and conquer.

To your success!!!

David.

www.ingramcontent.com/pod-product-compliance
Lightning Source LLC
Chambersburg PA
CBHW061237180526
45170CB00003B/1340